this is the beautiful life of

....

MY AUTOBIOGRAPHY IN DRAWINGS

my shoes

the contents of my fridge

*what I see when I open my eyes
in the morning*

my mailbox

what I wear to sleep

my front door

my favorite movie star

the contents of my wallet

a holiday gathering

my haircut

my favorite city

a uniform I've worn

my family tree

what I wanted to be when I grew up

my parents

the state I grew up in

my favorite food

how I feel about work

contents of my closet

my first bike

my favorite book

my first pet

 *where I socialize*

my spirituality

the person who cuts my hair

a time I went barefoot

what inspires me

my pants

 *my breakfast*

my first job

last thing I think about before
going to sleep at night

my school

my favorite music

my pen

how I feel about love

what makes me happy

my favorite childhood game

a baby in my life

where I work

 *my beverage of choice*

my bed

*my favorite childhood
birthday party*

my worst injury

where I hang out

my lunch

something that never fails
to make me smile

a body of water in my life

 *my first heartbreak*

 *a child in my life*

my phone

who I live with

my best friend

a story my parents tell about me

 *my face*

 *where I walk*

my first love

my favorite restaurant

 *my cousins*

 *what I think is mysterious*

how I feel about family

what I dream about

my hometown

my elbow

when I learned to drive

who I talk to on the phone

my computer

what I think is beautiful

 *my toothbrush*

my commute

nature in my life

me as a baby

my hobbies

what I splurge on

 *my eyebrows*

 *why I do what I do*

my first kiss

when I learned to dance

what I did after school as a child

 *my best vacation*

my kitchen

my favorite person

 *what makes me sad*

 *when I learned to swim*

my home

the weirdest thing
I ever ate

my favorite fruit

me as a child

the first magazine I read

something I like to make

 *a day I'll always remember*

my favorite candy bar

when I lost my first tooth

a party in my life

when it rains where I live

my favorite sweater

where my family comes from

 *what I got in trouble for*

 *the farthest I've been from home*

how I get from point A to point B

my town

my childhood fears

the best thing that's ever happened to me

 *my hands*

my creative outlet

where I'd like to live

 *my birthday*

 *a supposedly fun thing I'll never do again*

something I'm glad I tried once

my perfect day

*what I bought with my own
money as a child*

a chance I'm glad I took

someone I miss

 *how I feel about money*

how I'd like to be remembered

when I was most proud

my favorite breakfast cereal

my favorite landscape

a time I felt fearless

someone I'd like to meet

Library of Congress Cataloging-in-Publication
Data available.

ISBN: 978-1-4521-0853-7

Manufactured in China

Designed by Hillary Caudle

10 9 8 7 6 5 4 3 2

Chronicle Books LLC
680 Second Street
San Francisco, CA 94107

www.chroniclebooks.com